Contents

Animals

rabbit

Lots of animals live in the park.
The rabbit is one of Buster's favourite animals.
The rabbit lives in a burrow.
The burrow is under the ground.

burrow   grass   cabbage   car.rots

Dad - Buck
Baby - Kitten
Mom - Doe

Rabbits eat grass, leaves, cabbage and carrots.

20/02/06

2

The squirrel

red squirrel

There are squirrels in the park.
A squirrel builds its nest in a tree.
The nest is called a drey.
The squirrel has thick fur and
 a long bushy tail.

berries

drey

fur

bushy tail

nuts

Squirrels eat nuts, berries and fruit.

21/02/00

The fox

fox

Sometimes at night Buster sees
  a fox in the park.
The fox has thick fur and a long bushy tail.
Its tail is called a brush.

brush

hare

rat

The fox eats rabbits, hares and rats.
It likes to eat hens and ducks too.

The badger

badgers

There is a (badger) in a wood near the park.
The badger lives under the ground.
Its home is called a set.
The badger keeps the (set) very clean.

set

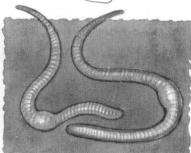

worms

grass

Badgers eat grass, berries,
worms and small rabbits.

27/02/06

5

The hedgehog

hedgehog

Another one of Buster's favourite animals
  is the hedgehog.
The hedgehog has spines all over
  its back and sides.
When it is in danger, the hedgehog curls
  into a ball.
Then it sticks out its spines.

snail

frog

spines

The hedgehog eats snails and frogs.

Buster Facts

 The hedgehog sleeps all through the winter. This sleep is called hibernation.

 The bat, the snail and ▲ the frog hibernate too.

 The squirrel only sleeps when it is very cold. ▶

2/03/00

7

Clothes

Emma comes to play in the park
  nearly every day.
Some days it is warm.
Some days it is cold.

jeans

shorts

coat

jumper

**We have clothes for warm days.
We have clothes for cold days.**

Clothes for cold days

When it is cold, Emma wears clothes
  which keep her warm.
She wears jeans and a thick woolly jumper.
She wears a thick woolly coat too.
Sometimes she wears a hat.

jeans

jumper

coat

hat

We get wool from the sheep.

07/03/06

9

Clothes for warm days

On warm days Emma wears light clothes.
Light clothes keep her nice and cool.
She wears shorts and a t-shirt.
Shorts and t-shirts are made from cotton.

shorts

t-shirt

**We get cotton from the cotton plant.
It is grown in hot dry lands.**

9/03/06

grey skirt

white shirt

Emma wears a uniform at school.
Her uniform is a red jumper,
a grey skirt and a white shirt.
All the other girls in the school
wear a uniform too.

red jumper

Some people wear uniforms at work.

9/03/06

Boots and shoes

Sometimes Emma wears boots.
Boots keep her feet nice and warm.
At other times she wears shoes.
When it is raining she wears wellies.
They keep her feet dry.

leather boots

leather shoes

wellies

Boots and shoes are made of leather.
We get leather from the skin of the cow.

13/2/06

14/03/06

Buster Facts

 The first people wore nothing on their feet.
Then people wore shoes
which were more like socks.
Later people wore shoes made of wood.

 Some clothes are made from linen.
We get linen from a plant.

Butterflies

butterfly

It was a hot sunny day.
Fergus and Alan were in the park with Buster.
There were lots of butterflies in the park.
They were going from flower to flower.

**Butterflies are found
all over the world.**

Nectar

Butterflies live on nectar.
They get the nectar from flowers.
The butterfly has a long tongue.
It uses its tongue to take the nectar
 from the flower.

butterfly

wing

tongue

nectar

flower

Some butterflies look like flowers and
some butterflies look like leaves.

20th/03/06

The story of a butterfly

butterfly

leaf

egg

The caterpillar eats and eats.
From time to time it grows a new skin.
Then it eats the old skin.

21/03/06

caterpillar

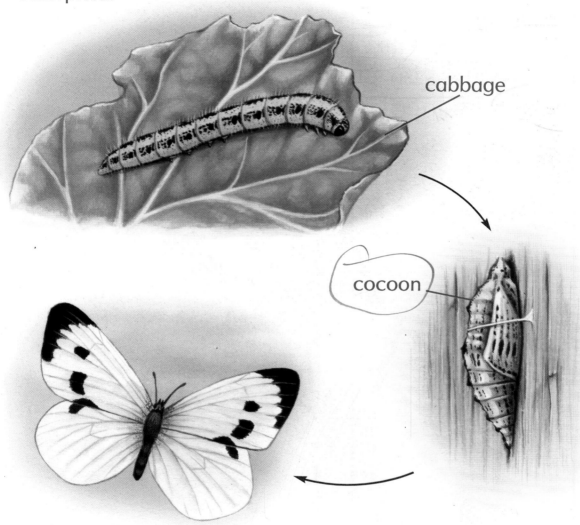

cabbage

cocoon

Some butterflies live for about a year.
But many butterflies live for just ten days.

22/03/06

17

Wings

When the butterfly comes out of the cocoon,
its wings are wet.
The butterfly sits on a leaf in the sun.
So its wings dry and grow longer.
Then the butterfly flies away.

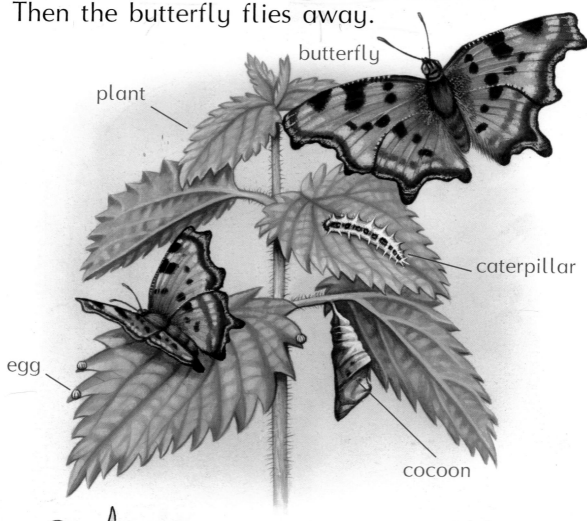

plant

butterfly

caterpillar

egg

cocoon

A butterfly can lay about 1000 eggs.

22/03/06

Buster Facts

Some butterflies stay in Ireland
all year round.
But some butterflies
come to Ireland
from other lands.
Some come from
as far away as Africa.

23/03/00

The airport

luggage

trolleys

Emma's Uncle Mike lives in London.
But from time to time he comes home
  on a visit.
Emma's Daddy always goes to the airport
  to pick up Uncle Mike.
Emma goes with him.

An airport is a very busy place.

At the check-in desk

Passengers check in their luggage at the check-in desk.

Looking down at the airport

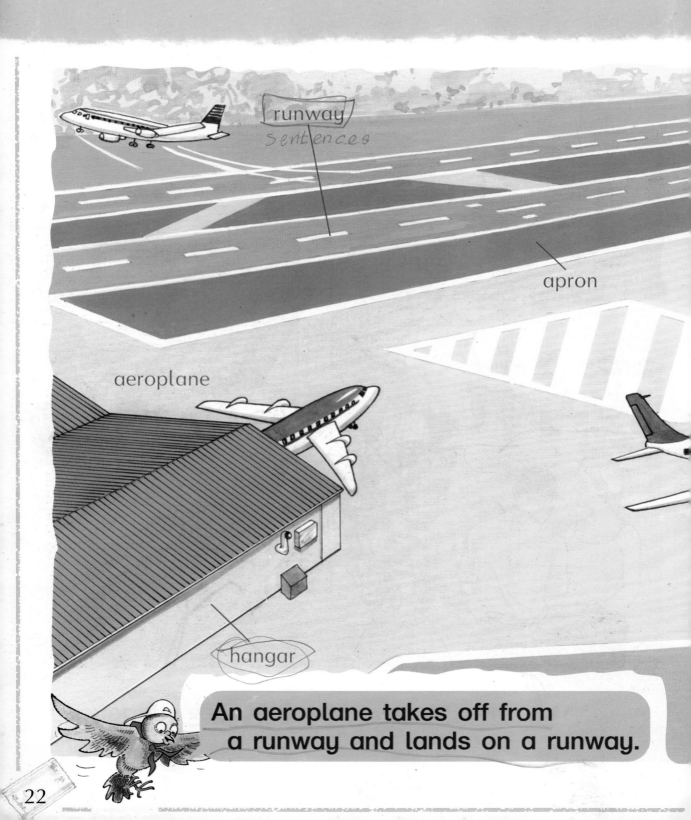

runway

sentences

apron

aeroplane

hangar

An aeroplane takes off from a runway and lands on a runway.

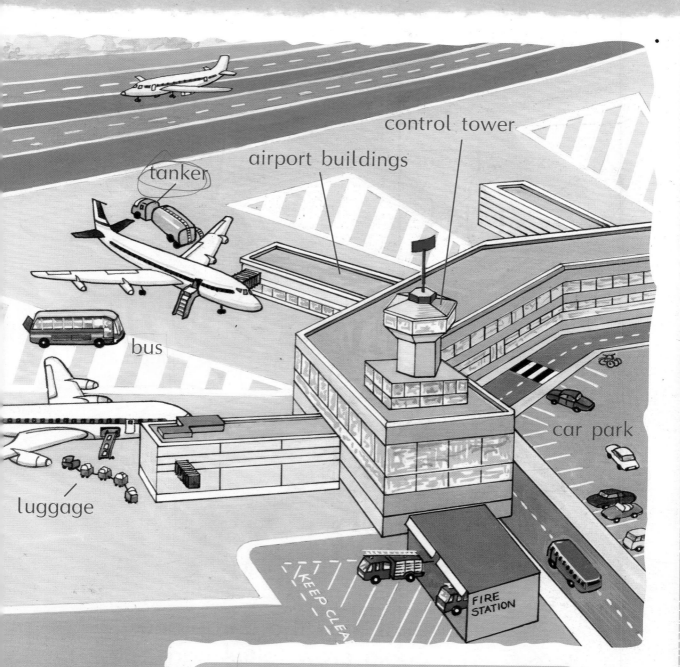

control tower

airport buildings

tanker

bus

luggage

car park

KEEP CLEAR

FIRE STATION

A hangar is a great big garage for aeroplanes.

28/8/08

On the aeroplane

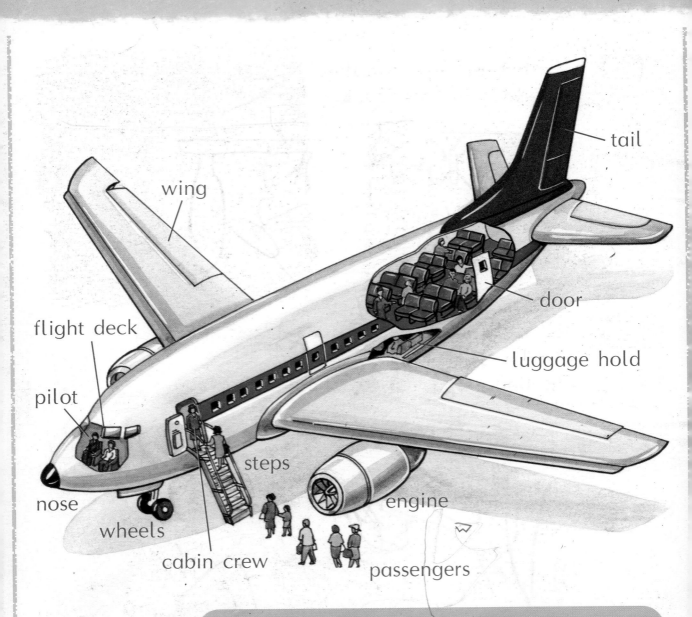

tail

wing

flight deck

pilot

nose

wheels

cabin crew

steps

engine

passengers

door

luggage hold

The pilot flies the aeroplane.
The cabin crew takes care
of the passengers.
The cabin crew is always very busy.

29/3/06

Buster Facts

The busiest airport in the
world is in America. ▶

▲
The first flight from America to Ireland
took place in 1919.
The tiny aeroplane crashlanded in a bog
in Co. Galway.

The first Aer Lingus flight was from Dublin ▲
to England in 1936.
The tiny aeroplane carried five passengers.

Bridges

There are two bridges in the park.
One is over the river and one is over the road.
The bridge over the road is a footbridge.
It is made of wood and is painted red.

Danger: deep water

footbridge

People can cross a footbridge,
but cars and trucks can't.

24/5/06

Stepping stones

stepping stones

At first people used stepping stones
  to cross rivers.
But stepping stones could be dangerous.
Sometimes people slipped on the stones and
  fell into the river.

Stepping stones could only be used where the water wasn't too deep.

Tree bridge

The first bridges were made from trees.
A big tree growing near a deep river
  was cut down.
Its branches were cut off.
Then the tree was placed across the river
  from one bank to the other.

The tree bridge could be made
bigger by using more trees.

29/5/06

Toll bridge

Sometimes people have to pay
to cross a bridge.
This helps to pay for the bridge.
The money is called a toll and
the bridge is called a toll bridge.

TOLL
2
EURO

toll bridge

The M50 bridge in Dublin
is a toll bridge.

30/5/06

Buster Facts

The longest bridge in the world is in America. ▼

What is a brige span?

The longest bridge span in the world is in England.
▼

There is a very big bridge in Scotland.
By the time one side of the bridge has been painted,
it is time to begin painting the other side.

31/5/06

Trucks

Orla's Daddy has a fishing boat.
He catches lots of fish.
He has a small truck too.
He takes the fish to the shops in his truck.
He puts ice in the boxes to keep the fish fresh.

windscreen

cab

Fresh fish

wheel

mirror

ORLA

Look at all the trucks.

6/6/06

Building a house

This man is building a house.
Look at all his trucks.
One truck is carrying sand.
Another truck is carrying blocks.
The big red truck carries cement.

Cement

cement

cement truck

sand

Cement is used to build houses.

6/6/06

On the farm

The farmer needs trucks too.
She uses the big truck to carry cows
 and sheep from place to place.
The green truck is for milk.
It is called a milk tanker.

wheel

milk tanker

mirror

**Milk stays cool and fresh
in a milk tanker.**

7/6/06

33

At the garage

This garage is a busy place.
A petrol tanker has brought petrol
  to the garage.
The break-down truck has brought a car.
The car has been in a crash.

petrol

petrol tanker

petrol

break-down truck

petrol tanker

We put petrol in our cars
  to make them go.

Buster Facts

The biggest dumper truck in the world
   was made in America.
It is about 17 metres long.

TRAILER

An articulated truck is made from two parts,
   a tractor and a trailer.
Some trailers are very long.

An Arab Sheik has the biggest caravan in the world.
It is 20 metres long.
It has eight bedrooms.

8/6/06

Sun and rain

One sunny day Emma and Alan came
to play with Buster.
They were running and jumping.
But soon they got too hot.
'Let's have some ice-cream,' said Emma.
'It's too hot to play.'

ice-cream

CAREFUL
CHILDREN

**Ice-cream can help to cool us down
on a hot day.**

12/6/00

The sun

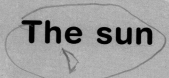

day

night

The sun is very far away from our world.
But it makes plants and flowers grow.
It gives us light too.
When it is day here,
   it is night on the other side of the world.

sun

clouds

stars

The sun is a great big star.

Sunburn

When we are out in the sun,
 we must always take care.
When it is very hot, the sun can burn the skin.
This is called sunburn.
Sunburn can be very dangerous.

sun cream

sun hat

sun umbrella

Always put sun cream on your skin
 when the sun is hot.
Always wear a sun hat too.

13/6/06

Rain

If it didn't rain, there would be
no rivers or lakes.
There would be no food to eat
or water to drink.
In some places it never rains.
These places are called deserts.

desert

sand

river

lake

stones

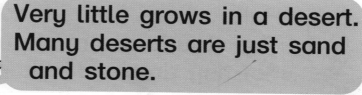

Very little grows in a desert.
Many deserts are just sand
and stone.

14/6/00 6

Clothes for rain

When it is raining, we can get very wet.
So we wear clothes and boots
  which will keep us dry.
We wear coats called raincoats.
On our feet we wear wellies or boots.
Some people use umbrellas too.

umbrella   raincoat

wellies   boots

Rain comes from clouds.
The clouds are made up
of tiny drops of water.

Buster Facts

 The biggest desert in the world is in Africa.
It is called the Sahara Desert.
The Sahara is the hottest place in the world.

The first umbrella was made about 250 years ago.
It was made by a man in London.
People used to laugh at him when they saw him
    carrying the umbrella.

15/8/06

Flowers

Emma's Daddy has a very nice garden.
It is always full of flowers.
He likes gardening.
He works in his garden every day.
Sometimes Emma helps him.

Flowers grow in fields and gardens.
Some flowers grow
in window boxes too.

22/6/06

How a flower grows

sun

heat

rain

petals

stem

leaves

root

Many flowers grow from tiny seeds.
The seeds are planted in the ground.
They need heat and water to grow.

27/6/06

The daffodil

The daffodil doesn't grow from a seed.
The daffodil grows from a bulb.
The bulb stays in the ground all year round.
The flowers come out in spring.
The daffodil has six yellow petals.

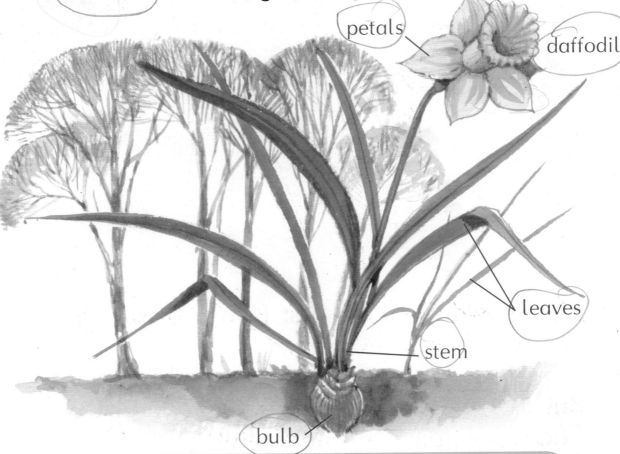

petals

daffodil

leaves

stem

bulb

Daffodils grow in wet ground.
They grow in gardens, parks and
on the sides of roads.

27/6/06

44

The snowdrop

snowdrop

leaves

petals

stem

bulb

The snowdrop is the first flower of spring.
It grows from a bulb too.
There can be snow on the ground.
But the snowdrop pushes up its tiny head.
The snowdrop has white petals.

**The snowdrop likes to grow
in wet ground and under trees.**

Buster Facts

 Some flowers close their petals at night. They open them up again in the morning when the sun comes up.

 Some flowers eat flies and butterflies.

Picture index

breakdown truck – page 34

drey – page 3

grey skirt – page 11

hangar – page 22

hare – page 4

heat – page 43

Picture index

nuts – page 3

rat – page 4

stars – page 37

Uncle Mike – page 20

wings – page 18

woolly jumper – page 9